Contents

Fiction
Spot the Difference
page 2

Play
Something is Different
page 22

Poem
In the Gallery
page 28

Non-fiction
Faking It
page 30

Written by
David Grant

Illustrated by
Rosy Higgins

Series editor **Dee Reid**

Before reading
Spot the Difference

Characters

Ash

Keri

Security Guard

Old Lady

Tricky words

ch1	p4	security	ch3 p12	crouched
ch1	p5	wandered	ch3 p15	politely
ch2	p8	realised	ch4 p16	swerved
ch2	p9	interrupted	ch4 p16	blaring

Story starter

Ash and Keri had to do an Art homework project so they went to the art gallery. The guide showed them a famous painting by Vermeer called *Girl with a Pearl Earring*. As the guide was talking to them, Ash noticed a security guard was staring at him. Ash decided there was something strange going on.

Spot the Difference

Chapter One

Ash and Keri were visiting the art gallery. They had an art history homework project to do.

"This is the world-famous painting *Girl with a Pearl Earring* by Vermeer," said the guide who was showing them round the gallery.

Ash wasn't looking at the painting. He was looking at a man in a dark uniform. The man was staring crossly back at him.
"Who's that man?" whispered Ash.
"He's a security guard," replied Keri. "These paintings are worth millions."
"Why is he staring at me?" asked Ash.
"Maybe he thinks you've stolen something," laughed Keri.

"Sshhh!" hissed the guide. She gave Keri a stern look.

"And over here," said the guide, "is another painting by Vermeer. It's called *The Music Lesson*."

Keri and Ash wandered over to look at the next painting.

Suddenly there was a loud thud. They all rushed over to see what had happened.

An old lady was lying on the floor. She looked very pale. Her eyes were closed. "Stand back," said the guide. She knelt down and held the old lady's hand. "It's okay," said the guide, "she's only fainted. She'll be fine in a moment."

The old lady opened her eyes.
"Where am I?" she asked.
Keri helped her to get to her feet.
Ash was having another look at the painting of the girl with a pearl earring.
He frowned.
Something was wrong. Very wrong.

Chapter Two

Ash kept staring at the painting.
Something had changed.
Suddenly Ash realised what it was. He called Keri over.
"Look," said Ash, pointing at the painting.
The security guard stepped forward.
"No touching!" he warned. "We don't want your grubby fingers all over our valuable paintings!"

Keri looked at the painting.

"We've already looked at this painting," she said.

"Look again," said Ash. "Something is different."

Keri looked puzzled.

"What are you talking about?" she asked.

"The girl in the painting is – " began Ash, but before he could finish explaining, he was interrupted by the shaky voice of the old lady.

"Excuse me," she was saying to the security guard. "Could you take me outside? I feel faint again. I need some fresh air. And could you bring my bag please?"

"Of course, madam," said the guard, picking up the old lady's bag. He took her arm and they headed for the door.

"Look at that old lady's bag," said Ash. "It's very big. I'm sure those two are up to something! Come on, let's follow them."
"You're being really weird!" said Keri.

Chapter Three

Keri followed Ash out of the gallery and into the car park.
Ash hid behind a litter bin. Keri crouched down beside him.

"What on earth is going on?" whispered Keri.

"The painting has changed because it isn't the genuine painting," said Ash. "That old lady and the guard have stolen the real one and swapped it with a fake. And now they're getting away!"

He pointed across the car park. The guard and the old lady were climbing into a scruffy bright yellow van.

"Quick!" said Ash. "I'll ring the police. You stop them."
"How am I supposed to do that?" demanded Keri.
"Just do it!" said Ash.
Keri hurried across the car park.
The yellow van screeched round a corner.
Keri shouted and waved at the van.
It skidded and came to a stop.

The security guard opened his window.
"What do you think you're doing?" he shouted.
"I think you've got a flat tyre," said Keri politely.
"No I haven't!" said the guard angrily.
"Look," said Keri, pointing at the back of the van.
The guard got out of the van and looked at the tyres.
In the distance a police siren wailed.

Chapter Four

The police siren got louder and louder.
"Get in the van and drive!" screamed the old lady. "It's the police!"
A police car swerved in front of the van, its lights flashing and its siren blaring.
A policeman and a policewoman jumped out of the car.

"Stop right there!" said the policewoman firmly. The policeman snapped handcuffs on the security guard's wrists. Then he got the old lady out of the van and put handcuffs on her, too.

The policewoman searched the back of the van.

"Well, well, look what I've found," she said.

"It's the *real* painting of the girl with a pearl earring!" said Ash.

"But he's a security guard!" said Keri. "He's meant to protect the paintings, not steal them!"

"He's not a security guard," said the policeman. "He's an art thief. His name is Barry Scrimm. We've been after him for years – and now we've got him at last!"

"And this," said the policewoman pointing at the old lady, "is his mum. She paints the fakes. Barry gets a job as a security guard in an art gallery. Then his mum comes in and pretends to faint. While everyone is taking care of her, Barry swaps the real painting with the fake."

"How did a couple of kids know it was a fake?" snarled the old lady.

"You painted it the wrong way round!" said Ash. "In the real painting, the girl is looking to the left. In your painting she's looking to the right."

"We could get ten years in prison because of you!" said Barry Scrimm grumpily.

"You two," said the policewoman to Ash and Keri, "will be getting a nice reward."

Quiz

Text detective

p4 — Why is it usual to have security guards at an art gallery?

p8 — Why does the guard not want Ash to get too close to the painting?

p15 — How does Keri show some quick thinking?

p18 & 20 — How can you tell that the police are pleased with Ash and Keri?

p19 — How did Barry and his mum work as a team?

Word detective

p5 — Which words tell you that the guide is cross with Ash and Keri?

p16 — Which verb tells you that the police car is moving fast?

What do you think?

Do you think Barry and his mum are any good at art forgery and theft? What things do they get right? What mistakes do they make?

HA! HA!

Q: Why did the man take a pencil to bed?

A: So he could draw the curtains!

Before reading
Something is Different

Characters

- Ash
- Keri
- Security guard

Setting the scene

Keri and Ash are visiting an art gallery for a homework project. Ash is looking at a famous painting called *Girl with a Pearl Earring*. A security guard is trying to get Ash to move away from the painting.

Something is Different

Ash: Keri! Come here.

Keri: What is it?

Ash: Come and look at this painting.

The security guard comes over.

Guard: No touching! We don't want your grubby fingers all over our paintings. They're worth millions.

Ash: I'm not touching it!

Guard: There are plenty more paintings for you to look at. There's no need to stand here pointing and poking at this one.

Keri: Come on, Ash! We've already looked at this painting. Let's look at the others.

Ash: No, wait. Have another look at this one. Something is … different.

Keri: What are you talking about?

Guard: Yeah, what *are* you talking about?

Ash: Nothing! *(whispers to Keri)* Look at the girl in the painting.

Keri: I *am* looking ... but what am I looking for?

Ash: She's moved.

Keri: Don't be silly! People in paintings can't move.

Ash: This girl has. A minute ago she was looking over her *left* shoulder.

Keri: And?

Ash: And now she's looking over her *right* shoulder.

Keri: Oh! You're right! I'm going to talk to that security guard. Excuse me, can you tell me when this painting was painted?

Guard: Hundreds of years ago, I think. Why do you want to know?

Keri: We looked at this painting a few minutes ago. There's something different about it now.

Guard: No, there's not!

Keri: The paint looks very new, don't you think? It looks almost as if … the paint was still wet.

Guard: I don't know what you're talking about. Now move along now you two. There are other people wanting to look at this painting.

Ash: Can you tell us how the girl was looking over her left shoulder a few minutes ago and now she's looking over her right shoulder?

Guard: Don't be silly. You're making a mistake. That painting has been here for years. The girl hasn't moved. Now buzz off before I call the police.

Keri: I bet no one could ever steal a famous painting like that, could they? Not with a good security guard like you looking after it.

Guard: Move along, you two. That old lady is looking over here. I think she could do with some help.

The guard hurries over to the old lady.

Keri: Hey!

Ash: I think they're up to something – him and the old lady. Come on, let's follow them!

Quiz

Play detective

- **p23** Which adjective does the guard use to suggest that Ash and Keri might spoil the picture with their fingers?
- **p24** Why is Keri surprised when Ash says the painting has moved?
- **p24** Why are the words 'left' and 'right' in italic type?
- **p25** How can you tell the guard is getting anxious?
- **p26** Why does Keri tell the guard that she thinks he's a good security guard?

Before reading
In the Gallery

Setting the scene

Imagine if the people in paintings could stare back at us! Imagine if a person in a painting could wink at us or escape from the frame and move into another picture.

Poem top tip

The first two verses are quiet like the gallery at night, but in the last verse when the figure has escaped there is movement and life. Try to read the poem creating first the stillness then the activity.

Quiz

Poem detective

- What surprises you in the second line of the poem?
- How would you feel if you saw a portrait in a gallery wink at you?
- What do you think the poet is trying to say about pictures and people visiting galleries?
- Do you think it is a sad poem or a happy poem?

In the Gallery

The visitors in the gallery stare.
I sit very still and very quiet in my picture
and stare back.
I sit very still
and when no one is looking
I wink.

But when the visitors have all gone
and when it's all gone very quiet
and when it's all gone very still
and no one is looking
I slip out of my picture
and into another picture.

And I dance in the fields
and feel the sun
on my back.

by David Grant

Before reading
Faking It

Find out about

- Why some people forge paintings
- What happened when the painting of Mona Lisa was stolen
- What can happen to people who forge paintings or diaries

Tricky words

p31	original	p34	museum
p31	forgeries	p35	Ancient Egyptian
p32	photographed	p36	diaries

Text starter

Forgers can make a lot of money by copying a painting then selling the painting, pretending that it was painted by the original artist. One forger painted copies of paintings that had gone missing so the galleries thought they were getting the original back. One forger pretended that some notebooks were Hitler's diaries!

Faking It

Making Money

Forgers can make a lot of money by making fake paintings. Forgers copy a painting, then they sell the copy, pretending it was painted by the original artist. Sometimes, forgeries are so good that only art experts know if they are real or not.

Stolen!

The painting of *Mona Lisa* is in a gallery in Paris. Experts think it is worth nearly £500 million. In 1911, *Mona Lisa* went missing. The security guards thought the painting had been taken away to be photographed – but it wasn't being photographed. It had been stolen!

Some people believe *Mona Lisa* was stolen by a forger. They think the forger wanted to make and sell copies of the painting. He would pretend that each copy was the real painting. Nobody knows what really happened. The painting was missing for two years. Then it was given back to the gallery.

Caught!

One art forger was very successful.

He found out about paintings that had been lost or gone missing. Then he painted a copy of the missing painting. His parents took the fake painting to a museum or a gallery to try to get them to buy it. They told the staff at each museum that they had been given the painting by a relative.

The forger made a lot of money from the forgeries.

He was even successful in fooling the British Museum. He sold an Ancient Egyptian statue to the museum for £400,000. The museum staff did not know that the forger had made the statue at home!

When the police caught the forger, he was sent to prison for more than four years.

Hitler's Diaries

It's not just paintings that forgers copy and sell.

In 1983 a man sold 60 notebooks to a German magazine. He said that the notebooks were Hitler's diaries and that they had been found where a German plane had crashed at the end of World War 2. The staff at the magazine believed him and they paid more than £3 million for the diaries.

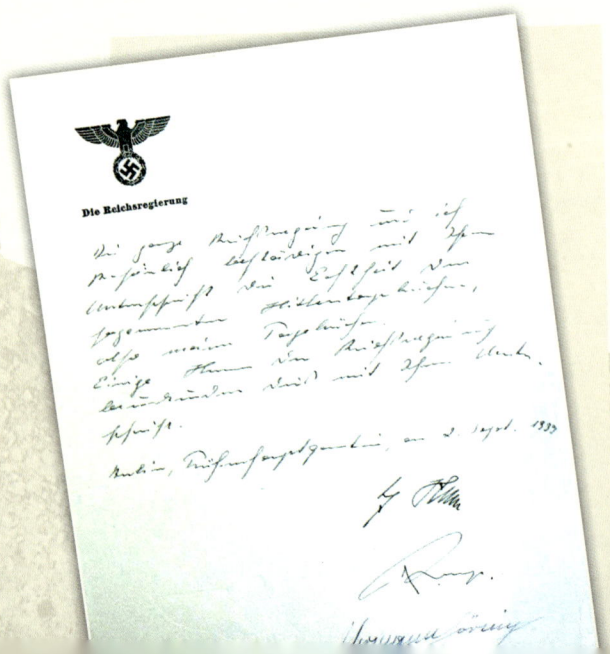

But the man was a forger, and the diaries were not very good forgeries. The magazine staff should have been able to find out that the notebooks could not be Hitler's diaries. The forger had used modern paper and ink that did not exist when Hitler was alive!

The forger was sent to prison for more than four years.

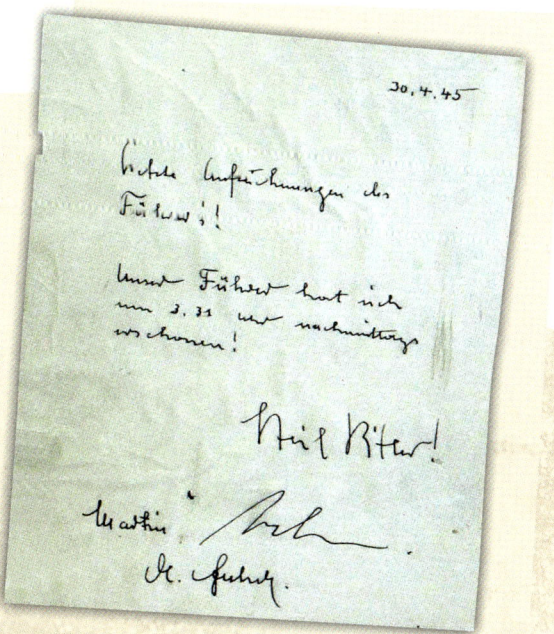

Fake Potter

In the UK you can read 7 different books about the wizard Harry Potter – but in China you can read lots more. That's because in China there are lots of Harry Potter books that were not written by J K Rowling. They are written by Chinese writers who pretend that J K Rowling wrote the books!

Quiz

Text detective

- **p31** How do some forgers get away with it?
- **p32** Why were the security guards not concerned when the Mona Lisa painting was missing?
- **p35** How do you know that the forger of the Egyptian statue was a good forger?
- **p38** Why are there more than seven *Harry Potter* titles in China?

Non-fiction features

- **p32–33** Think of a subheading for these two pages.
- **p35** Why does the author use an exclamation mark at the end of the first paragraph?

What do you think?

If the forger can trick a gallery into thinking that a painting is an original then should it be as valuable as the original? Why do you think forgers are sent to prison? Do you think that is fair?

HA! HA!

Q: Why did the artist have to go to jail?

A: Because he was framed!

Published by Pearson Education Limited, a company incorporated in England and Wales, having its registered office at Edinburgh Gate, Harlow, Essex, CM20 2JE. Registered company number: 872828

www.pearsonschools.co.uk

Pearson is a registered trademark of Pearson plc

Text © Pearson Education Limited 2013

The right of David Grant to be identified as the author of this work has been asserted by him in accordance with the Copyright, Designs and Patents Act 1988.

First published 2013

19 18 17
11 10 9 8 7 6

British Library Cataloguing in Publication Data is available from the British Library on request.

ISBN: 978 0 435 15241 3

Copyright notice
All rights reserved. No part of this publication may be reproduced in any form or by any means (including photocopying or storing it in any medium by electronic means and whether or not transiently or incidentally to some other use of this publication) without the written permission of the copyright owner, except in accordance with the provisions of the Copyright, Designs and Patents Act 1988 or under the terms of a licence issued by the Copyright Licensing agency, Saffron House, 6–10 Kirby Street, London ECIN 8TS (www.cla.co.uk). Applications for the copyright owner's written permission should be addressed to the publisher.

Designed by Bigtop
Original illustrations © Pearson Education Limited 2013
Illustrated by Rosy Higgins
Printed and bound in China (CTPS/06)
Font © Pearson Education Ltd
Teaching notes by Dee Reid

Acknowledgements
We would like to thank the following schools for their invaluable help in the development and trialling of this course:
Callicroft Primary School, Bristol; Castlehill Primary School, Fife; Elmlea Junior School, Bristol; Lancaster School, Essex; Llanidloes School, Powys; Moulton School, Newmarket; Platt C of E Primary School, Kent; Sherborne Abbey CE VC Primary School, Dorset; Upton Junior School, Poole; Whitmore Park School, Coventry.

The publisher would like to thank the following for their kind permission to reproduce their photographs:

(Key: b-bottom; c-centre; l-left; r-right; t-top)

Alamy Images: © Lou Linwei 38; **Bridgeman Art Library Ltd:** Giraudon 33, Vermeer, Jan (1632-75) 28; **Getty Images:** 31, Gamma-Rapho 34-35, Getty Images 36-37; **Veer/Corbis:** Brenda Carson 29

All other images © Pearson Education

In some instances we have been unable to trace the owners of copyright material, and we would appreciate any information that would enable us to do so.